FINANCE

What Your Parents Never Told You About Money

Money Management, Budgeting & Investing

By Jason Preston

Table of Contents

Chapter 1: Start building your wealth with your first paycheck 9

Chapter 2: Emergency Funds 21

Chapter 3: Saving and Being a Frugal Spender 29

Chapter 4: Know Where Your Money Is Going 41

Chapter 5: Building Your Credit and Controlling Your Debt 49

Chapter 6: The safest way to invest your money: "The Three Buckets Rule" 63

Chapter 7: Investing like a millionaire 69

Chapter 8: Increasing Your Income 79

Chapter 9: Creating Passive Income 91

Conclusion 107

Bonus 111

Introduction

This book is intended as a guide for people who are looking for a basic and easy way to control their finances. It is not a comprehensive guide, and will probably have to be modified a bit to your specific needs, but it will give you a general idea of the fundamentals and habits needed to achieve financial freedom – now and in the future, without giving up on the things you love. This book is designed in a way to get you to take action and get you started on your path to financial freedom.

The most important part is doing all of this in such a way that you don't go without. By controlling how you spend money, you won't have to give up on that five-dollar cup of coffee, new album download, dress or pair of shoes. This is not a book about depriving yourself until you are retired, that's just boring, and then having a little fun when there's only a few years left! Instead, I believe there is a way where you can have your cake and eat it, too. I'm not a financial expert, but these tip and tricks that I'm going to give will more of a case study on what I do and what works for me – and others.

Along the way, I will try to debunk various financial myths that may hold you back and provide tips and tricks that can help you move forward in your life so you can achieve financial freedom no matter what your income level is now.

So if you're ready to stop being broke, start controlling your finances – instead of having them control you – then let's turn the page and find out **What Your Parents Never Told You About Money**:

Chapter 1

Start building your wealth with your first paycheck

Before we start, I want to give you a word of encouragement: anybody can be a millionaire if they really want to be. America is the land of opportunity where anybody can start with nothing and end up on top of the world. In fact, most of the people who made themselves into millionaires actually started out with nothing. So if you're thinking to yourself that I can't do it, I'm struggling to make ends meet, I'm in debt, I'm telling you now that you can.

I'm going to give you one of the biggest secrets all millionaires and billionaires know that the average person never even think about, it's a simple rule that once you master it, it will make all the difference to your life (really no bull I do this all the time). Here it is: **pay yourself**

first. One of the most important habits that you can create in order to reach financial freedom is to learn how to pay yourself first. Sounds simple enough, but ... what does it really mean and, more importantly, what do you need to do? Paying yourself first simply means that you must be sure to first pay your monthly savings contributions – what you want to put away for "yourself" every week – by the time you receive your pay check and, instead of borrowing on credit or from your savings, then live your life using the remaining amount. In other words, pay yourself as if you were a bill every month, the rest of your money will then go to everyone else.

To achieve your financial goal, you should learn to discipline yourself and spend your money on the most important things only, or the things that you need most. Here's a simple example of what I mean: Let's say that Tommy gets paid $1,800 a month working at a fast food restaurant. Since he gets a weekly pay check that comes out to about $450 per week.

Now, Tommy has a few bills, which are:

• $100 for his cell phone payment;

• $40 for liability car insurance payment;

- $150 school payment;

- About $180 a month in gas;

- His rent is $350 for a room (with roommates);

- $200 a month on food (Tommy's on the rice bean and top roman diet)!

Add it all up for a grand total of $1,020 a month. Given that his monthly pay check is $1,800, this means that at the end of the month Tommy has $780 left over **after his bills**. Tommy's goal is to save (i.e. "pay himself") at least $200 a month or about 10% of his income. He puts away $50 into his savings.

So, here is a four-week plan to help Tommy "pay himself first, before the daily, weekly and monthly expenses that fritter away at our hard earned dollars creep up and tempt him to spend his money elsewhere:

The First Week

- Tommy receives his $450 pay check;

- He immediately deposits $50 into his savings account;

- He spends $45 in gas to fill up his tank;

- He spends $100 on the phone bill;

- This leaves Tommy $255 left over as spending money for the week.

The Second Week

- Tommy receives his $450 pay check;

- He immediately writes a check for $350 to cover rent (Sadly, this week almost all of Tommy's check will go to rent. Sorry, Tommy!)

- He still has to pay $45 for gas to fill his tank for the week.

- This only leaves Tommy $55 left over for the week.

The Third Week

- Tommy receives his $450 pay check;

- He immediately pays himself first by depositing $100 into his savings account to make up for last week where he couldn't put away $50;

- He subtracts $45 for gas;

- He subtracts $150 school payment

- This leaves Tommy with $155 leftover as spending money. (That's a lot better than last week!)

The Fourth Week

- Tommy receives his $450 pay check;

- Pays himself -$50

- As usual, he spends $45 for gas;

- He also has to write a check for $40 for car insurance;

- optional -$100 to his saving

If you're keeping score, this leaves Tommy with between $215 and $315 of spending money left over after he pays all his necessary bills and pays himself by putting money away in savings every week. It isn't always easy for Tommy. Look at the one week where he only has five bucks to spare! These are the times when "paying yourself first" might seem like a real drag, but just think about what that money can do for you as it accumulates over time! After a while of doing this your stress level goes down you have a stash of money you're not dead broke, know you're building wealth!

What to Do Now

At first, this will take a little discipline to deduct that weekly savings deposit to pay yourself first, but after a while this it will become a habit – a rule of thumb – to make sure you're on track is to make sure the numbers in your account are growing the numbers are getting larger! Sometimes you'll lose discipline on this and you'll notice your account hasn't changed at all. If the number aren't growing, you're doing it wrong and you need to make some changes so that the numbers in your savings account go up, not down. Remember, doing this right will set you up to have money to make more money, which we'll cover in other chapters.

Tip: Go to the ATM or the bank pull out the money you give yourself to spend leave the money your saving alone in your bank account, this will help you plan purchases better and force you to not touch your savings. I'll explain more on this in a later chapter.

• I recommend reading *The Richest Man in Babylon* by George S. Clason (Stellar Editions, 2014) this book will give you a general idea on the of paying yourself first and wealth building

Achieving Financial Freedom

Before we get any further into this book let me talk about creating a financial freedom plan. None of this book will matter if you don't have a set plan. You know people wake up every day to go to work, get paid, get days off, then start the process over again. Booooring! If you have a plan, even if it's a simple one, that alone will set you apart from about 95% of all the people out there.

I believe that the simpler the plan is the easier it will be to take action on. The financial freedom plan should be basic so it's easier to process in your mind and easier to take action. The first step is simple: make the decision, right now, today, that you will be financially independent and you will be able to overcome all the obstacles in your way. I'm telling you now; this is not going to be easy. But if you start every morning by reminding yourself of your decision, you are going a long way towards achieving financial independence. You will face a lot of obstacles towards achieving your goal, but if you persist, you will be successful.

Another important thing that you need to do is to develop a financial vision. Ask yourself, where do I want to be financially five years from now or ten years from now? Do I want to have a new house? A new car? How much money do I want to have in my bank account? Having a vision of where you want to be in the future helps motivate you to save money and better manage your finances. Don't be afraid to dream big and make your vision as seemingly unreachable as you can. After all, if you dream it, you can achieve it.

You can also create financial visions for the short-term and the medium-term. For example, your financial vision for the next month might be to have $1,000 saved up so you can take a nice vacation with your family. Or if you have a credit card bill that has been bothering you, you can resolve to pay it off by the next billing period.

But to make it easier for your financial visions to come true, you might want to subject them to the SMART test. Is your vision Specific, Measurable, Achievable, Relevant and Trackable? If your vision passes this test, then you can surely make them into a reality!

Write down your financial visions on a piece of paper and then, when you wake up first thing in the morning, review them. Think about how close you are to achieving your visions as well as what you can do to bring yourself closer to making it a reality. If necessary, you can re-write and adjust your financial vision as you change your mind about what you want to achieve.

When you're doing this exercise, it is very important that you talk to your spouse about it. After all, you should be on the same page as far as sharing your financial vision is concerned. You might end up pulling in opposite directions if your financial vision is a new house and your wife's is a new car! If you can, you should write down your financial vision separately, and then exchange them. Afterwards you can talk about what you've written down so you can agree on what your joint financial vision is.

Another important thing to talk about in order to avoid friction is your attitude towards money. The way we feel about money actually determines how we spend it. For example, have you ever wondered why you feel it is perfectly okay to spend $5 on a cup of latte coffee but you think that putting aside $10 a month for savings is too much of a sacrifice? The answer, of course, lies in your values and what you feel is important to you. So you should take some time to think about how you feel about money. This might involve some painful self-reflection as well as looking back at your past to determine why you feel the way you feel about spending on certain things. You might discover for example that you don't like to save because your mother always told you that it was a waste of money.

In addition, there are also things that you can do for self-improvement that would help you get closer to achieving your financial vision. For example, you can start every morning by planning your day in advance. This would greatly help you to become more focused and more self-disciplined. If you know what you have to do and what you have to finish during the day, it becomes easier for you to resist temptation and say no to that expensive cup of Starbucks coffee.

You can also program your mind for financial success by reading books and listening to podcasts about financial success. There are many books and audio programs that you can consume that will teach you how to become wealthy. You can get up earlier every morning and spend at least one hour reading. Depending on how fast you read, you can finish a book in around a week. This means that you would have read fifty books in a year.

If reading books is not your thing, then you can listen to audio programs on your way to work. If you spend a lot of time commuting or driving to work, you can spend the time wisely by listening to these programs on your iPod or mp3 player. Many people have used audio programs to learn how to make more money and increase their knowledge.

Finally, end your day by asking yourself two important questions before you go to sleep: what did I do right? And, what would I do differently? You should also ask these questions after finishing something important such as a meet or a sales pitch. By asking yourself these questions you are forced to examine how you performed on that day or that important occasion. There are many lessons you can learn. At the very least, you can discover how to do better the next time or the next day.

Chapter 2

Emergency Funds

Ok so you're saving money now and that's good, but what are you saving for? What's the next step? Let me break it down for you like this, the fact of the matter is that life happens. We sprain our ankle skateboarding and can't work for a few weeks. Or we get laid off, or sick, or downsized, or the business we work for closes down. Then what? Where does our money come from until we get better – or find another job?

One of the ways true wealth is usually measured is by asking yourself a simple question: "How long can you survive your current lifestyle without needing a pay check?"

An "emergency fund" is your answer. An emergency fund is the cornerstone of making life easier, and less stressful, financially speaking. When we're constantly at the "red line" with our bills – living pay check to pay check, not much in savings, always borrowing money and never able to pay it back – life can get very stressful. And when you can't pay a bill on time, you'll be penalized with late fees, which can add even more stress. But with an emergency fund, you can get ahead of the game by being able to pay your bills on time, and even ahead of time.

Things can get even worse when there is a sudden unexpected expense that we don't have the money to cover. What if your car breaks down, and you need it to get to work? You'll be forced to use your credit card to pay for the repairs, and when you can't pay off the balance in full, you'll be deeper into debt. Or what if someone in the family gets sick and has to go to the hospital? Will you have enough money to foot the bill?

With a good emergency fund in place, however, you feel more secure and less anxious all the time. And while it may sound challenging, creating an emergency find is really quite simple.

So, what exactly *is* an emergency fund? Basically, you're going to want to set a particular number of months where you can say to yourself, "Okay, if I'm out of work or not getting paid for this long, I can still pay my bills and have enough to eat!"

In other words, you're going to want to save enough money to live for about three to six months without getting a pay check. Or, if you really want security, twelve months' worth of savings makes for an excellent emergency fund. I know it sounds like a lot, but the fact is you already have the tools to do this. How? By using the techniques of paying yourself first that we talked about in Chapter 1, you should already be in the process of making this happen.

The first step to creating an emergency fund is determining the amount you need to save; the second step is in saving it! First things first: How do you know how much to save?

Let's revisit our old pal "Tommy" again as an example. As you'll recall, when you look at his rent, bills and other "fixed" expenses that are due regularly, Tommy needs about $870 a month. Now, remember, we're trying to determine how much to save if we want an emergency fund for, say, three months, six months and twelve months. So let's run some numbers for each of those:

- **$870 multiplied by three months would be $2,610;**

- **$870 multiplied by six months would be $5,220;**

- **12 multiplied by twelve months would be $10,440;**

- **And so on...**

As you can see, those are some pretty stiff figures! However, since Tommy knows how to pay himself first – and so do you – the framework is in place if he can just convert that knowledge into action and begin creating his emergency fund.

What to Do Now

Now it's your turn: determine what your outstanding bills are every month – the things like rent, food, electric, cable and other things you'd need to survive – and determine how big your emergency fund might need to be to last you three months, six months and an entire year!

Once you've done this exercise and you know how much you need to put aside for your emergency fund, how can you save up the money? Here are some suggestions for strategies that you can follow:

Break down your savings goal into smaller ones. If your computations tell you that you need to save around $10,000 as your emergency fund, that can seem pretty daunting. But if you break it down into smaller amounts, it can be less discouraging. To illustrate, instead of telling yourself you need to save $10,000, start by saving $1,000 first. Give yourself a deadline for achieving this – say around six to twelve months. Once you've saved $1,000, set another goal of saving $1,000. Keep on doing this and in time, you'll eventually have a big emergency fund.

You can also create a long-term plan to save for an emergency fund. For example, you can decide to save the $10,000 over three or five years. This means that you'll need to save $278 a month (for the three-year plan) or $167 a month (for the five-year plan).

Give yourself time to set up your emergency fund. It takes time and a lot of patience to save a big amount of money, so you should not get discouraged. Also, don't lose hope if you can only save a small amount at a time. Even if you can only put aside $10 every week, at the end of the year you would have $520, which can be of great help if an emergency arrives.

Set up a separate savings account for your emergency fund. Doing this will help you avoid the temptation to dip into it when you get a little short of money. There are many options for opening your emergency savings account. For example, you can open an online savings account that will prevent you from easily withdrawing your money. However, if you would like to earn some interest while building up your emergency fund you can consider options such as a money market account that allows you to withdraw starting at a minimum level or a short-term savings certificate with a three- or six-month maturity term.

Set up automatic debit. You can open an online savings account and then ask that a certain amount be deducted from it every month and put into your emergency fund account. This will make savings easier since you are automatically doing it without having to think about it. And, of course, if you don't see it, you can't spend it!

To make building up your emergency fund quicker, you can look for ways to save money that you can put towards it. Here are some suggestions:

Ask your credit card provider for a rate reduction. If you've been paying off your credit card debt religiously and your account is in good standing, try calling the customer service number on the back of your card. Ask for a supervisor and then request that your interest rate be reduced. Tell them that you're considering transferring your balance to improve your chances.

Shop around for lower insurance rates. These days, it's easier than ever to compare insurance rates. Simply log onto an online broker site and ask for quotes. Or if you're willing to do more work, visit the sites of individual insurance providers and request quotes. Then switch to the insurance company that gives you the best deal.

Avail of discounts on your auto insurance. You may not be aware of it now, but there are many discounts that car insurance providers offer that can save you money on your rates. For example, some companies will cut your rates if you take a class on defensive or safety driving. Other discounts that may be available include those for having low mileage on your car, installing safety devices and having a good driving record.

Reduce the use of your car. You can save money on gas and other car costs by using public transportation to go to work if it is available or by organizing a carpool with your neighbors. Even if you don't use your car only once or twice a week, the savings can really build up over time. There'll also be less wear and tear on your car, meaning that you'll able to save on maintenance costs as well. Or if you live close to work and want to get some healthy exercise, it might be practical for you to bike to work.

Use your windfalls well. If you get an unexpected bonus or your tax refund arrives in the mail, don't be tempted to spend it all on unnecessary things. Treat yourself a little, but save the bulk of the money. Better yet, check how much tax is being withheld from your salary. The IRS actually recommends that you do every year or after every important life event such as getting a new job or a second job, getting married or buying a new home. While this means that you will not be getting that big tax refund check every spring, it also means that you are saving money now that you can put aside towards your emergency fund. In addition, it helps you avoid nasty surprises from the tax man later on. After all, you might end up actually owing tax without knowing it instead of getting a refund.

Chapter 3

Saving and Being a Frugal Spender

I know. I know I said in the begging of this book you can build financial freedom and still have the things you want, but there still has to be a bit of sacrifice. Frugality isn't what a lot of people think it means (being cheap); being frugal means spending your money on the things you really want vs the things you don't care about. For an example, we all want a cell phone right? But do we really need to pay a high phone bill? No! Ask yourself; do I text more then I make phone calls? Make your plan as cheap as possible by paying for less minutes that you don't use or even if it means paying off your device (if you're doing the payment plan) to get as low as possible. This will free up more money and you'll still have the phone you want.

I know it can be hard to justify saving money when we barely have enough to live on in the first place, but here's a simple statement that might put things into perspective for you: **<u>Saving money is just as important as making money</u>**. I like to think of it this way: If you pouring water into a bucket with to money holes you will never have any to drink.

Think about that for a minute: we tend to put our focus on making money and ignore what we spend. But when we spend less – i.e. save money – the money we make goes further.

So the focus shouldn't always be on just making more money, but on spending less for the things we need. Ask yourself, "How do you spend your money?" In other words, you can still get the things you want but that doesn't mean you always have to pay full price for things.

Let's say you set aside twenty dollars a week for entertainment. For you, entertainment means going to the movies. Typically, you spend your entire twenty dollars on one movie a week. That's not hard to do these days; movies are expensive!

Let's break it down to see how that $20 gets spent:

- **Movie ticket: $10**

- **Large popcorn: $5**

- **Large candy: $3**

- **Large soda: $2**

Well, that's no fun! But that's the way you've always done it, so that's how you keep doing it. But there are ways to have the same experience and not spend quite as much. For instance, a matinee ticket between 4 and 6 PM costs $7, and the theater runs a special where tickets are $5 all day, every Tuesday. By switching what time, or day, you go to the movie, you could cut your expense in half – and see twice as many movies! Instead of buying a large everything, buy a medium and save yourself five bucks, or buy smalls and save yourself ten bucks, etc.

Learning about money is not just saving yourself a couple of bucks once, but getting into the habit of finding ways to spend smarter every day so that the money you do make goes farther and provides more options.

So learn to decide where your money will be spent each month. Which "Bucket" are you filling this week/month? Put the right amount of cash that you will need for the month into the right places. Separate some money into each of those three buckets we talked about: Security, Growth and Dreams. With this method of separating your cash, you can control and determine the right direction for your money and avoid spending it unwisely.

And over and above all that, learn to save money wherever – whenever – you can. For instance, sites like Groupon.com can help you buy the things you like... for less. For example, using Groupon I was able to bring down my cell phone bill for two people to $110 a month from $200.

Here are just some simple ways you can learn to spend less on the things you're already using, like and enjoy:

• **Learn to negotiate.** We've already talked about negotiating for lower insurance rates. But you can also try calling other service providers to see if you can do the same thing. For example, with cord-cutting an increasing problem for cable providers, if you really can't live without it, call them and ask if they can lower your rate. Try this also with your Internet provider, etc. Remember, the worst they can say is "No".

• **Do the math.** Learn to compare different plans to see which one gives you the better value. If you're going to buy a DVD rental plan, for instance, don't immediately go with the one that has the lowest rental. Check out what other perks and benefits you can get. You might save more money in the long run from the perks even if you have to pay higher rental charges.

- **Research things that matter to you.** Let's say you like to listen to music, watch movies and play games in your "media room". It would help to have one streaming service that provides all your needs, at the most reasonable cost. How can you have a device that lets you watch Netflix or another streaming service, listen to Pandora or Spotify and play games? Could it be an app or Amazon Prime or an Xbox live gold membership? Study up on the best, most affordable service and then look into it so that you can have all of your entertainment needs for less.

- **Spring for the warranty.** Get a warranty on devices whenever possible, as they help prevent big expenses in the future. Remember that if your device breaks down after the warranty has expired, you'll either have to pay for the repairs out of your own pocket or replace it. That small additional expense you're paying now might save you more money in the future.

- **Cut out the waste.** When you look over your expenses, look for areas where you may be wasting money. For example, if you have a subscription to a magazine that you don't actually read, cancel it. If you are a member of a streaming service but you realize that you're only watching a couple of hours a month, you might want to consider renting DVDs instead of paying a monthly subscription.

Here are some more handy tips on how to save money:

- **Get rid of your vices.** Are you still smoking or drinking? While it may be hard for you to get rid of these addictions, it might help if you count how much money you're wasting on these vices. For example, WalletHub estimated that, based on the state you're living in, a lifetime of smoking (around 51 years) can cost you anywhere from $786,300 (in South Carolina) to as much as $1.5 million for Alaskan residents. Just think of what you could do with that money!

- **Avoid impulse spending.** The next time you go to the supermarket, sit down first and make a list of the things that you actually need to buy. Then take the list with you and stick to it! Don't buy anything that does not appear on the list.

- **Save the difference.** One way that you can trick yourself into saving is to budget too much for an expense and then saving the difference. For example, if you normally spend around $350 to $370 for groceries in a month, you can budget $400, then save what you don't spend. You can also try this trick with other expenses.

- **Avoid visiting stores when you're stressed.** Many people deal with stress by spending money on stuff they may not really need. So you might be better off finding other ways to blow off stress such as spending time with friends, watching funny movies or even meditating or exercising.

- **Cut down on sweets and junk food.** This is another area where you may be shocked at how much you are spending. Apart from the money savings, you'll be healthier since eating too much of this stuff is not good for you.

- **Save your change.** Every little bit helps, so take the change that you've collected during the day and put it in a jar. Do this everyday and then count how much you're saving at the end of the month or year. You might be surprised at how much you've saved. In addition, you can tip yourself for a job well done so that you can add more change to the jar.

- **Take care of your stuff.** In order to ensure that your appliances last longer and don't need to be replaced before their time, you can perform simple maintenance tasks. For example, you can dust them to prevent the dust from getting into the works and damaging them. In addition, these appliances will run more efficiently and save you money on your electricity bills.

- **Repair and recycle.** Instead of throwing away clothes that are slightly damaged, repair them if you can. It might be a good idea, if you're serious about saving money, to learn how to sew and perform small repair jobs.

- **Buy used instead of new.** One way that many people have used to save money is to frequent the Goodwill and other used goods shops and buy used clothes and other second-hand stuff. A lot of these things are as good as new but were simply thrown out or donated by people who didn't want them anymore, so you might as well benefit from them.

- **Shop for the holidays in advance.** Don't wait until the last minute to do your Christmas shopping. Shop way before the holidays when prices are cheaper. In addition, you can save money by shopping after the holidays, when many stores drop their prices in order to get rid of unsold inventory.

• **Buy generic.** Next time you're in the supermarket, instead of buying the usual branded products, try the generic or house brands. These offer you the same quality, but at prices that are much lower.

• **Get rid of stuff that you're not using.** If you have clothes in your closet that no longer fit you or that you no longer wear but are still good, why not sell them off? You can have a yard sale or sell them online. You can even donate them to charity and get a tax deduction.

• **Don't waste heat.** A programmable thermostat can help save money on heating bills by ensuring that the heat is turned down when no one is at home. You can also program it to regulate the temperature while you're sleeping.

• **Don't let lighting burn a hole in your pocket.** Switch the lights in your house to more energy-efficient LEDs or CFLs. While you may be paying more for these bulbs, you'll enjoy more savings in the future as your energy bills go down. In addition, you'll save on replacement costs since these bulbs last much longer than ordinary ones and don't need to be changed as often.

• **Maintain your car.** There are simple things you can do to ensure that your car is running efficiently and thus, use less fuel. For example, you can clean your air filter or change it as needed. You can also check that your tires are at the proper pressure. These little things can greatly improve your car's fuel mileage and save you hundreds of dollars over its life.

• **Bring lunch to work.** Wake up a little earlier in the morning and prepare your lunch instead of buying at the cafeteria or food cart. While it would be ideal if you did every day, even cutting down twice or thrice a week can save you a lot of money over time.

As you can see, there are many ways to save if you simply take some time and see the value of spending less on the things that matter to you most. One final tip: use cash more often. It's easy when using credit cards, or even your cash card, to spend more because you have a little "cushion" with whatever is in your account. But cash is a finite amount: if you only have forty dollars in your wallet to spend, that's all you'll spend. It's a way of making your weekly "budget" real and, more importantly, sticking to it!

It's more inconvenient, I know, but that's the point. The harder you make it on yourself to spend, naturally, the less you'll spend. So if you constantly need to go to an ATM or to your bank to get cash, it makes it a little harder to spend money. This simple trick makes you think twice before spending. You also need to plan your spending better and, with the cash in your hands, you want to make it last so you tend to make better choices when spending. Finally, you'll spend less on things you don't want.

What to Do Now

Now it's your turn: find one simple thing to give up this month. It could be changing your premium music subscription service like Spotify or Pandora to a less expensive option that plays ads, or finding a less expensive way to stream movies or download music, whatever. Just find one thing to cut out this month – and every month – until you start to chip away at your monthly expenses.

Chapter 4

Know Where Your Money Is Going

There's a simple truth about money that I think is important to share with you now: if you don't control your money, your money will end up controlling you. For instance, if you make $2,000 per month but have $1,500 in bills, you're really only left with $500 per month for spending money. However, if you only had $1,000 in bills, you'd be left with $1,000 per month – nearly twice the original figure. Are all those bills really necessary or can you eliminate some of them?

Therefore, to achieve your financial goals, you must learn how to control your expenses so that you have more money to work with every month – and more financial options available to you.

One way of controlling your expenses is by creating a personal budget. A budget is essentially a listing of everything you spend in a month that tells you where your money is going so that you'll know where you can cut down. Budgets can also help you save for financial goals like a vacation, a down payment for a new house or car, etc. as well as helping you get out of debt.

The first step in creating a personal budget is to list down all your expenses. There are two ways you can do this. You can gather all of your bills and then list down what you're spending on, or spend the next month listing down everything you spend. Whichever method you use, what is important is that you are able to capture as much of your expenses as you can. To make it easier to compute how much your expenses are you can set up a spreadsheet on Excel or other similar programs.

Once you've listed down as many of your expenses as you can, it's time to compare them with what you earn. If you are a salaried employee, use the amount you take home after deductions for tax, your 401 (k) contributions and so on. If you are self-employed, simply add all the income you get from all sources.

Compare your income with your expenses. If there is an excess, then you're doing great! On the other hand, if your spending exceeds what you earn, you're in trouble. You're probably in debt, and things are only going to get worse. Creating a budget is now more important than ever for you.

Now it's time to create your budget. There are several approaches you can take based on why you are budgeting.

For example, if you are saving, then you can put the amount that you want to save as the first expense category in your budget, and then allocate the remaining amount of your disposable income among the remaining categories.

To illustrate, let's go back to our old friend Tommy. We've already established that he earns $1,800 a month and has $820 in fixed expenses (for rent, his cell phone bill, school payment and so on) plus spends $200 in food. In addition, he wants to save $200 a month. This means that he only has $780 left over to budget. A rough budget could look like this:

Spending Money = $780

    Food = $200

    Clothes = $--

Leisure = $--

Personal Expenses = $--

Of course it depends on you what your particular expense categories will be. But the point of this budget is to know where your money is going so you won't fritter it away and you can have more control over your spending.

There are other approaches to budgeting that you can take. For example, there is the 50/30/20 plan. Under this plan, you will allocate 50% to living expenses, 30% to leisure and other lifestyle expenses and 20% for long-term savings (such as saving for retirement or big expenses such as a new house or car). Under this plan, your budget would look like this:

Spending money = $780

Living Expenses = $390

Lifestyle   = $234

Long-term Savings = $156

It is now up to you to decide how to allocate the amounts for living expenses and lifestyle spending.

The major benefit of having a personal budget is that it lets you see, in black and white, just where your money is going so that you can make adjustments. For example, are there any areas where you may be spending too much? Is there waste that you can get rid of so that you'll have more money to spend on what you really need? In addition, a budget allows you to play around with your money, allocating more to the things that are really important to you and spending less on things which you can do without.

If you're trying to get out of debt, a budget is a great tool. Since you can see how much you have to spend, you can treat debt payments as a fixed expense, and then reallocate the remaining amount once you've removed it from your spending money.

But, you should not look at the budget as a way of depriving yourself of the things that you really want; instead consider it a way of focusing your spending so that you can get more from your money. This is why you should not panic and start cutting back too quickly when you see that you are spending too much on certain things.

For example, if you realize that you are spending way too much on lattes, you don't need to remove them from your budget at once. Instead of having a latte daily, you can cut down to only twice a week, for example. Don't set yourself up to fail in your budget by cutting out everything that you find fun in your life. Give yourself a little money for small luxuries and indulgences.

Finally, you should not be too hard on yourself when you go over your budget. Life can sometimes throw you a curve ball, and you may end up spending more than you intended in a month. If this happens, don't get too frustrated. Tell yourself you'll do better next month.

What to Do Now

Now it's your turn: create your own personal budget. Start by making a list of all your monthly expenses. Look for areas that you may be wasting money on and eliminate them. For example, do you have a gym membership that you may not be using?

You should also look at the small expenses that you may be taking for granted but which add up to a big amount over time. If you are drinking a can of soda a day or smoking a pack of cigarettes, you may be saying to yourself that they are not that expensive. Try to add up how much you are actually spending for them in a month or a year and see how much money you're actually wasting. But don't be too harsh on yourself; have a little fun, just not too much!

Chapter 5

Building Your Credit and Controlling Your Debt

Not all debt is bad. For instance, let's say you want to open up a side business (more on this later) mowing lawns in your neighborhood. You don't have enough saved up to buy a new lawnmower, but you can buy one on time at a local hardware store. This kind of debt allows you to earn extra money and, once it's paid off for in regular installments, is no longer a monthly liability.

Then again, using your credit cards to buy things you don't need – tons of music you've downloaded, new clothes you'll never wear, junk food and sneakers and so on – doesn't necessarily add to your earning potential.

So, depending on your purpose for borrowing money, there is "good" debt and "bad" debt. Regardless of what kind of money you're borrowing, you must learn how to spend it wisely.

But, remember that credit is not always bad. In life, there are times when you will need to make expenditures that help improve, not worsen, your financial situation. For instance, a digital camera that helps you take pictures of items to sell on eBay or Etsy can pay itself off in a few transactions, qualifying as good debt.

So building your credit is not bad as you think – *if* you can learn how to handle and use your credit card(s) wisely. Actually, credit can be a convenient and safe way to transact everywhere and anytime when you don't have enough cash in your wallet.

Use your credit only on the things that you really need and don't spend beyond your credit limit, so you can have a good credit history. If you are planning to apply for a loan at the bank, your credit history is important because one of the things that they look at is your credit report to determine whether they will give it to you and what interest rate to charge you.

How to Improve Your Credit

The first step in improving your credit is knowing where you stand. Request a copy of your free credit report/s. You are entitled to one free report a year from the three major reporting agencies – Experian, TransUnion and Equifax – meaning you are entitled to three reports in all. All you have to do is visit the Annual Credit Report site and fill up a short online form. Make sure you get a copy from all three agencies since there may be items that are not included in one report that may be included in the others.

Once you have received your credit reports, it's time to review them. These reports essentially provide a snapshot of how you use credit. The information they contain is also used to compute your credit score, which is one of the factors that lenders use to determine if they will give you a loan and under what terms they will extend credit to you.

What's in your credit report? Here are the major sections:

• Credit accounts. This section reports on all the loans you have taken out from lenders (mortgage, credit card loan, auto loan, etc.), as well as what the credit limit is, the amount of the loan, how much is your balance remaining and your payment history (how regularly you make payments, if you pay on time, etc.).

• Credit inquiries. This section lists everyone who has asked for a copy of your credit report over the past two years. It includes 'voluntary' inquiries (those that were made because you applied for a loan) and 'involuntary' (those that were made by credit card companies offering 'pre-approved' cards).

• Public records and collections. This section contains information gathered from collection agencies as well as state and county courts. If you've declared bankruptcy or there is a judgement against you, that information will appear here. This section also includes information on overdue debt that was already sent to collection agencies.

If you are serious about getting your credit situation under control, you might also want to invest some money in getting your credit score. Credit scores are not free; they cost $20 from the My FICO site, but they provide you with a lot of information that may be useful to you.

What is a good credit score? Credit scores have a range of 300 (lowest) to 850 (highest). The higher your score, the more creditworthy you are to creditors. However, the credit score is not the only factor that lenders look at when considering whether to extend you credit and the terms that they will provide, since they will look at all the information on your credit report.

Now that you have your credit reports, it's time to look them over and find areas where you can improve your credit. Here are some of the problem areas you need to correct:

• Late/Delinquent Payments. Your payment history represents 35% of your credit score, making this area one of the most important to address if you want to improve your credit. Make sure that you pay your bills on time since being even a few days late can hurt your score if collections have started. If you already have late payments on your record, you can fix your credit over time the longer you pay promptly; but you should accept that the problem will not be easily repaired. If you have problems paying off your bills promptly, you should set up an automatic debit arrangement with your bank so that money will automatically be taken out to pay for them.

• Balances owed. This area makes up 30% of your credit score and is more easily managed. The best way to keep your scores down in this category is simply to keep the balances on your credit cards low. If you already have high balances, try to pay them off as quickly as possible instead of opening new accounts to move your debt around, since having fewer accounts is better for your credit score. Look at the next section below for strategies on how to pay off your credit card debt.

• Having several credit cards or installment loans that you manage responsibly will do more for your credit score than closing several credit cards that you don't use or opening new accounts. Having no credit cards at all and dealing only using cash would also not help. After all, it is important to demonstrate to potential creditors that you know how to manage your credit. Not having any credit cards might signal to them that you don't know how to use credit and make it more difficult for you to get a loan.

• One practice that you should avoid, however, is maintaining several credit cards that have small balances. Instead, pay off these balances and limit yourself to one or two cards that you use for all your purchases.

Another important thing to consider when looking at your credit reports are errors. There are many reports that show that errors in credit reports are very common occurrences. So if you have otherwise good credit, you should look for erroneous entries in your reports. Here are some of the most common things to look out for:

• Credit information that is not yours. While a lot of errors involving personal information are basically harmless, like for example if they misspell the name of your street, others are more serious. If you have a common name, you might find that information belonging to another person with the same name is mistaken for yours. This can hurt your credit score if your 'name-alike' has bad credit.

• Incorrect payment status. There may be open accounts still listed in the report that you have already paid off or accounts still listed as delinquent even though you have already started to make payments on time.

• Identity theft. This is a more serious issue, since this means that someone has been able to get your credit card information and other personal information and used it to make charges against your card. If you see accounts that are not yours, you should immediately contact the credit card companies to notify them as well as the credit reporting bureaus so they can freeze your accounts.

If you find any errors, what you need to do is list them down. Then prepare a letter to send to the credit agency that prepared the report where the error occurred as well as the organization (store, bank, etc.) that reported the erroneous entry. List the items that you want to dispute, making sure that you clearly identify them so they can easily be found. It would greatly help if you enclose a copy of the report with the mistakes circled. Then explain why each entry is erroneous, stating the facts to support your claim. Finally, ask for a correction.

When you send the letter, make sure you use certified mail and request a return receipt so you'll know that it has been received. When you send a letter to the organization/creditor, ask them to send a copy of the letters they send to the credit bureau. The agency is required to either delete the erroneous items within five business days after it gets your letter or reinvestigate the items.

If the agency chooses to reinvestigate, it must finish within 45 days after it received your dispute if you sent it after you received your credit report; otherwise, it must complete it within 30 days. Once it has completed the reinvestigation, it must notify you within five business days after it finished and send you a revised credit report if they made changes.

How to Pay Off Your Credit Card Debt

If you are staggering underneath your high credit card bills, don't despair! Here are some ways in which you can pay them off. Of course, it won't be easy and it will take time, but with patience and effort, you can do it!

First, let's look at the two common strategies that are used to pay off credit card debt:

1.   Pay off the card with the highest interest rate first. The idea behind this strategy is that you are paying a lot of money on interest charges so you should target the card that has the highest rate. The way it works is, you should only pay the minimum on your other cards and then make additional payments on the card you are targeting. Once that card is paid off, then pay off the card with the second highest rate, using the savings from having eliminated one of your accounts to make extra payments, and so on. Once you pay off a card, the money you would have spent on interest can be put towards the other balances.

2.   Pay off the card with the lowest balance first. Using this strategy can greatly provide you with a psychological

boost since you will feel that you are making progress in eliminating your debt. First pay off this balance, while still paying off the minimum on your other cards. Once you've finished with one card, use the savings to target the card with the next highest balance, and so forth. Many people who have used this method claim that it really works.

Now the question is, how can you raise money to pay off your credit cards? Here are some of your options.

• Borrow from a peer-to-peer lender. While it may seem weird that you are borrowing money to pay off your credit card debt, this makes sense if the interest on the peer-to-peer loan is lower than those of your cards. The major benefit of these loans is that they have fixed rates which are usually around 20% to 30% lower than those of credit cards.

• Use your savings. If you already have an emergency fund established, you can use the money that you were intending to save towards paying off your credit card debt. This can save you more money in the long run since you will be paying less expensive interest. In addition, since interest rates on ordinary savings accounts are low, you will end up saving more from eliminating the interest you are paying on your loans.

• Balance transfer. This is an option that you should consider carefully, since the terms under which the transfer is offered can be deceptive. In this option, you transfer your credit card balances to a single card that has a lower or zero interest rate for a certain period. However, after the introductory low rate term is finished, you may end up with higher rates than on your old cards. Thus, if you choose to avail of a balance transfer, make sure that you can pay within the introductory period. Also, don't charge anything else on this card while you're paying off your balance. In addition, make sure that you change your ways since many people who have availed of balance consolidation have found themselves facing the same debt problem since they continue to live beyond their means and accumulate new debt.

• Refinancing your mortgage. This is another risky strategy since it basically involves your having to take out a second loan against your home. When you already have paid off a certain portion of your home, i.e. if your house is worth $250,000 and you've already paid off $100,000, this amount is called your 'equity'. The bank may allow you to take out an additional loan against this equity so you can pay off your credit card balances or consolidate other debts. You may be able to get the same interest rate as your first mortgage or if you get a higher rate, set up the due date of the second loan so it matches the first one so that you can combine them when they need to be renewed at the best interest rate. However, you should not do this on your own and should consult with a debt counselor or other financial professional first.

What to Do Now

Now it's time to start thinking about credit a little differently. Ask yourself:

- Do you have a credit card?

- Or more than one?

- What are their balances?

- Do you have enough credit for your needs?

- How can you pay down credit when it gets out of hand?

Answering these questions will determine not only how much credit you need, but how to keep it under control.

Chapter 6

The safest way to invest your money: "The Three Buckets Rule"

When it comes to reaching your financial goals, sometimes it can help us to think differently. Typically, when we think about saving, we picture putting money into bank accounts. But what if there was a better way to save money that would allow you to more clearly visualize where you want it to go? In this case, why not try the "Three Buckets Rule"?

Under this method, you will establish three buckets, each of which will hold money for a particular financial goal. While you can designate whatever financial goal you want, here are suggestions for the three buckets:

1.) The Security Bucket

As we've just seen, sometimes in life, you have to deal with various challenges, emergencies or stumbling blocks. For example, your car can break down, or you can be involved in an accident. Even worse, you might lose your job. To be able to deal with life's challenges successfully, you have to develop financial security.

Financial security means that you can go to sleep at night without worrying about whether or not you will have enough money to meet your needs for tomorrow. It also involves knowing that you have enough to cover emergencies as well as meeting your future financial goals. For example, do you have enough money to be able to retire in comfort?

One way to plan for financial security is with a Security Bucket. Your security bucket would include money that you want to put aside for short- and long-term savings as well as your emergency fund. For example, you might want to save money in the bucket so that you can establish an Individual Retirement Fund that you pay for yourself.

2.) The Growth Bucket

Growth is a part of life, and definitely a part of your finances. Even if you have a good job or are earning a decent income, you should not rely on your salary alone. It is important that you look for ways to grow your money so that you'll have enough to cover emergencies, improve your lifestyle and be able to retire without worry.

In future chapters we will talk about how to grow your money – a part-time job, a night job, a weekend job, side jobs, passive income, etc. This bucket would hold the money you want to put aside to grow your finances, whether it is used to start a small side business, make small investments and so on. For instance, you might want to put money in the bucket so you can purchase a few shares of stocks that pay dividends, then roll over the dividends so you can buy more shares and so on to grow your stock holdings.

3.) The Dream Bucket

Finally, here is where you put aside the money for a particular dream, goal or passion you might have. Everybody has something that they've always wanted to do but was never able to because they didn't have the money to fund it. For instance, maybe you want to become a dancer but dance class is out of your budget right now.

This is why the Dream Bucket is important. You know that if you put money into this bucket, you can one day afford dance lessons – or piano lessons, or to take a dream cruise or buy a digital camera to feed your photograph habit, etc.

Of course, the three buckets don't literally have to be buckets – they can be envelopes that you put money in or separate savings accounts that you open. But what is important is that you treat them as bills that you pay to yourself. You can decide to put in a fixed amount each week to every bucket, or a percentage of your income. You might decide to allocate 5% of your salary to your Security Bucket, another 5% for your Growth Bucket, and 2% for your Dream Bucket.

Or you can schedule when you will put money into a particular bucket. For example, you can put money into the Security Bucket during the 1st week of the month, then put money into the Growth Bucket in the 2nd week, then into the Dream Bucket in the 3rd week and so on. Thus, you are ensuring that every three weeks each of the buckets has money put into it.

What to Do Now

Now it's your turn: think about the financial goals that you most want to achieve, then establish buckets for them. You can even make your goals more specific. For example, instead of a Security Bucket, you can call it the Emergency Bucket or the Savings Bucket. Instead of the Growth Bucket, you can call it the Business Bucket and so on.

Once you've established your buckets, pick a bucket to put money into each week. Get in the habit of "rotating" your buckets every week so that you're always putting something into one of them, but never neglecting any of them. It's the obvious choice to choose security or growth over our dreams, but dreams are just as important – that's why there's a bucket for them, too! What is ultimately important is that you make it a habit to regularly 'feed' your buckets.

Chapter 7

Investing like a millionaire

Don't let your money sleep in the bank (see next chapter as well). Aside from the income you earn from your job, there are other ways to make your money work for you and increase your income. For instance:

• You can buy real estate and earn income from the rental property.

• Investing your money in the stock market gives you greater chances of growing your money.

• You can open an online store and create marketing around it that drives traffic even while you sleep.

These are all examples of what is known as 'passive income'. Before we discuss this concept, let's try to differentiate the three types of incomes first. These are:

Active or earned income. This refers to any income that is acquired or generated by working or by active effort. Therefore, as long as you spend time and effort on an activity and you earn from it, it is called active or earned income. Examples of this type of income are the following:

- Earning a salary from having a job.

- Making money from having a small business.

- Earning a fee from consulting.

- Receiving commissions from selling.

Active or earned income is the most common way that most people make money. However, the biggest downside of this type of income is that once a person stops working, the money stops coming too. Another disadvantage is that the amount of time and effort being spent on active income usually leaves no extra room for other income-generating activities.

Also, when it comes to tax matters, this receives the highest rate. The personal tax rate can range from 10% to 35%. This is not all there is to this unfortunately. Active income is also subject to social security and Medicare taxes. Add all these up and one would be left with only around 50% of gross earnings.

Portfolio income. This refers to any income that is generated by trading or buying and selling investments such as:

• Paper assets – this includes stocks, mutual funds, bonds, T-bills, forex and others.

• Real estate – buying and selling of properties.

• Other assets – examples are cars or antiques, which you can buy and sell for a profit.

There are two ways of earning money from portfolio investments:

• By trading the investment. The portfolio investor buys the investment at a certain amount and then sells it once the value appreciates. The most common example of this is investments in financial instruments such as stocks and foreign currency, where the investor waits until the value of the asset goes up and then liquidates his holdings. But this can be done with any asset. For example, real estate investors may buy a run-down property at a cheap price, refurbish it, and then "flip" it since the renovations have increased its value.

• By collecting the income generated from it. For instance, some stocks pay dividends, which are some of the profits of the company that are shared with investors. T-bills and bonds pay interest once their term expires and the investor redeems them.

As with earned income, portfolio income comes with disadvantages, too. These are:

• Trading paper assets require knowledge and experience. Those who are interested to try this must spend time and effort in understanding the process or else, he might get burned. Instead of earning money, he can lose a lot of money.

• There are always risks involved. The investor has little control over his investments. For example, there is a risk that the asset that you are buying will lose value rather than increasing in it. The company issuing a stock, for example, may experience business problems or even go bankrupt, thus making their stock lose value or even become worthless. Other types of market instruments such as forex may also experience wild fluctuations in price, thus causing investors to lose money on their investment. Hence, it is advised that you should not invest money that you are cannot afford to lose. If you have extra money that you wouldn't mind losing, then go ahead and invest.

• An initial cash amount is required to start. You need to have a certain amount of investment capital in order to start investing. If you don't have enough, then the amount of investment you can make may not be worth it since it will not generate enough of a return on your money. For those who follow the "pay yourself first" rule, you can use this money to invest, after you have saved up for your emergency fund, that is.

• The taxes, depending on the type of investment, may also be high. Long-term investments are taxed with lower rates. You should be knowledgeable on tax matters too so that you can maximize the benefits of portfolio income.

• Portfolio income is a long-term investment strategy. For example, most investors who hold stock keep it for a longer period of time since most of them don't greatly appreciate in value over the short-term. Material assets such as antiques also usually take a long time before they become more valuable. Thus, for those who are expecting a quick payoff or who want to generate a regular income stream, this may not be the ideal way to invest your money.

Portfolio income is promising but it is not easy. Hard work is necessary. Plus, for those who are not risk takers, this might prove challenging for them.

Passive income. This refers to earned income with little or no effort exerted or required on you. This means that the main role of the investor is to just invest or place money on something and it brings back money for him. There is no active participation required from you, as the investor. This gives you more time for other things like jobs, businesses, or family matters. Examples of this are:

Self-charged interest – this is when the investor lends money to a partnership or S-corporation, in which he is also a part or member of that corporation. In some scenario, this would not apply, such as when the member/owner earns as much as 100% from the corporation. Other than this, he could save a lot of money from tax exemptions. Hence, it is important to know the different tax laws that would apply that could lessen the tax rates for the individual and the business, as a whole.

Rental properties – You earn this type of income by buying a property specifically to rent out to qualifying tenants. However, you have to be sure that the amount of rent that you charge is enough to cover the loan payments on the property while still allowing you to make a profit.

It is also important to remember that a rental property is not totally a passive investment since you will still have to manage it. For example, it is your responsibility to maintain the property as well as taking care of the tenants' concerns. If there are any repairs that need to be made, it is up to you to complete them or hire somebody to do so.

Business income – Not all types of business income qualify as passive income. If you are actively involved in the business, for example, this would fall under the category of earned income. But a business like a vendor machine would not require too much of your time and effort, hence this is a type of passive income.

Affiliate or multi-level marketing – this is a marketing strategy where a person earns not only for his actual sales but also from the sales of the "downlines" that he has created. Downlines are the people that he has recruited to join the team and be under his leadership.

This can be considered a form of passive income since you can continue to earn even if you are not selling, since you are earning a specified commission from the sales of the people you've recruited. Of course, you have to make sure that your downline continues to actively sell in order for you to earn passive income from them, and this requires you to regularly meet with them for progress reports and to encourage them to continue selling.

Intellectual property – this is creating and selling items that originated from one's creativity. For example:

• Writing books and earning from selling them.

• Composing songs and earning royalties.

• Obtaining patents for inventions. You can produce the invention and sell it, or you can sell the rights and earn royalties from the sales.

• Making YouTube videos and other online content and monetizing it. The most common way of monetizing videos is by selling ads that will play before the video or in the middle of it.

Peer-to-Peer lending. If you have extra money to spare, you can consider lending it out to help other people in need. All you have to do is sign on to a P2P platform, where you can fund loans with a minimum investment of $25. Of course, you will have to take on more risk, but you can also enjoy higher returns.

Dividend-paying stocks. This is a good way to profit from stocks since you are getting paid a certain amount for as long as you continue to own them. Dividends are generated from part of the earnings of the company issuing the stock, and you can use the money to buy more shares or put it in your bank account. This is a better long-term strategy for building savings for the future rather than as a passive income technique, but you can also use it to earn recurring income with minimal effort.

What to Do Now

Now it's your turn: learn more about passive income and what it can do for you. Search the term on the internet and begin to explore more fully the world of passive income so that you can truly "make money while you sleep". There are many resources that are available to you online, ranging from blogs to podcasts, where people who have successfully generated passive income share their secrets.

Chapter 8

Increasing Your Income

Value: The simple truth about earing more (as cliché as it sounds) is giving more. Increasing your value is the only way to making more.

Many of us spend what we earn, with little thought given to saving money, increasing our income or planning for our future. If we make $1,000 a month, we generally spend that – or more – using credit cards to make up the difference.

I'm sure I don't have to tell you that is no way to finance the lifestyle of your dreams. In fact, that's making a beeline straight to a life filled with debt. If we want to finance our dreams and goals, we need to take a look at ways to increase our income.

Remember, having a job or running a business is a means to an end. In short, they are vehicles for you to receive financial gain. Every paycheck, every month, every year is an opportunity to grow your finances – just like a business would – and get wealthier every year. We often look for that one big "payoff" but the fact is wealth accumulates in little ways every day rather than the big "homerun".

So we're not looking for ways to win the lottery but, instead, how to increase our income in ways that add value a little at a time. This doesn't necessarily mean getting a new job, a better job or even an extra job. Increasing your income is all about increasing your value. This can be done in a variety of ways, such as:

• **Educate yourself.** There is always a class to take to increase your value. You can take a computer class, an accounting class, a class in social media or human resources so that whatever you are already doing, you will be able to do better and whatever you currently don't know how to do, you will soon know how to do. By upgrading your skills, for example, you will be able to qualify yourself for greater responsibilities in your workplace. You can also keep yourself relevant by constantly updating your knowledge so that you can easily adjust to the changing requirements of the job marketplace.

• **Train yourself.** You can also gain knowledge during weekend seminars, reading self-help or how-to books, attending local networking meetings, joining business groups, listening to inspiring speakers, etc. Anything you can do to train yourself will add value to your work and life. It is important to keep in mind that constantly learning is not just about increasing your value and making yourself more valuable to employers. Gaining knowledge for knowledge's sake can also greatly add value to your life, helping expand your horizons and enhancing your life.

• **Apply yourself.** Start where you are and apply yourself at your current job. Promotions and raises are ways to increase your value while staying where you are. Simply working an extra hour every day could mean big payoffs in overtime, a promotion or even a raise, and is something you can do while you're already on site. Show that you are dedicated to your job and your superiors will surely take notice and reward you.

• **Reinvent yourself.** You might want to try something new, like starting a side business to earn income on the side. You could start at Etsy store and sell your crafts, write an eBook and sell it on Amazon.com or turn your hobby for landscaping into cold, hard cash during evenings and weekends as you cut lawns and landscape around your neighborhood. You don't need to feel trapped by whatever course you completed in college or what job you've been doing for the past several years; if you want to change course and embark on a new career or become self-employed and start a new business, you can do so if you are determined enough and willing to work hard.

Starting a Side Business

Another way to increase your income is by starting a side business. Once upon a time this meant mowing lawns or delivering papers or setting up a lemonade stand, but now the internet makes it easy for nearly anyone to start a virtual store create extra income. Think about things you're passionate about, like movies or jewelry or fashion or music, and try to make money off them.

I started an online business at handmade crafts, which gave me an extra $200 a month. It doesn't sound like big money, but over time I kept adding to my savings and investing accounts and turned that small profit into big gains.

Here are some tips if you're interested in starting your own side business:

Ask yourself: What am I passionate about? When choosing a side business, the first question you ask should not be, what will make money? Instead, what are my interests? What do I love to do in my spare time? Once you've answered these questions, you can then ask: How can I make my interests into a business?

For example, if you love to cook, why not start your own small food cart or home catering service? You can create your own specialties to make your business stand out and, eventually, grow your business.

It is important to remember when starting a side gig that you should pursue your passion, not the money. If you are not really interested in your side business but are doing it just because you think it will earn, why bother? In the end, it will probably not be worth it.

On the other hand, if you are really engaged with your side gig, then it will likely make money, one way or another. After all, passion can be infectious and your customers can sense whether or not you are genuinely interested in what you are selling to them.

Don't spend too much at first. Many side businesses actually cost very little to start out. In fact, many experts say you can start one with just an initial investment of $100 or even less. However, you should not spend too much when you are starting out since you are still testing your idea to see if it will be successful. And if your side business costs too much at the start, then you should probably think twice about it, since you may be risking too much money on an untested venture. If it fails, it could leave you badly in debt.

Don't be afraid to experiment. As long as you keep your risks low, there is no reason why you should not try out new ideas in your side business that have not been done before. Even if you feel that there is not much of a market for your side business, you should still try it as long as you don't spend too much. You might tap into the next big thing by accident.

At the same time, however, you should not rely on the novelty of your business to sustain it. You have to be sure that what you are offering is always providing a valuable service to your customers.

Learn how to manage your energy. If you have a full-time nine-to-five job as well as a side gig, it can be hard to find the time and energy to devote to both. So it is very important that you learn how to manage both your time and your energy. For example, you can devote whatever spare time you have, including lunch breaks, to your side gig. You can also create more time by waking up an hour earlier than you usually do.

In addition, you can also find more efficient ways of doing necessary daily tasks, such as chores. Instead of going to the grocery, for instance, you can order your groceries online and have them delivered so you can have more time for your side business.

To get more done, however, you should learn to manage your energy. If you're a morning person, for example, wake up earlier and work on your side gig early in the morning, when your energy is at its highest. Find the time when you are most productive and use these times to maximize your productivity on your side gigs.

In addition, it is important that you take care of yourself. Make sure that you take care of your health by getting enough sleep, eating the right food and having a regular exercise routine. After all, what's the using of having a successful side gig if it makes you sick and you end up with substantial health expenses?

Don't lose focus on your customers. One of the most important things to remember when starting a side business is that you should always serve your customer's needs. Thus, you should be regularly seeking feedback from them about what they want from your business. Doing this can not only help make your business profitable, but save you money as you don't waste valuable resources creating products or services that no one is interested in.

Learn from your mistakes. When you launch your business, you should expect setbacks, and prepare yourself for them, emotionally, financially and psychologically. If you are not ready for business reversals, then you will not survive and will easily give up.

You should keep in mind that many of the most successful people in business today repeatedly suffered setbacks before they achieved their current status. They did not let failure deter them, and neither should you.

Adjust your definition of success. A side gig does not have to earn a lot of money in order for it to be considered a success. As long as it generates some income for you and makes you feel fulfilled, then it is successful. And even a small profit can help make ends meet or, if you reinvest it wisely, grow over time to become a big amount.

Be aware of your tax responsibilities. As a small business owner, it is up to you to compute how much tax you have to pay on your earnings, as well as how much you can deduct. Thus, you have to familiarize yourself with the IRS rules about your particular business. In addition, you have to be organized enough to keep your financial records in order so that you'll be able to justify your deductions on your tax returns. If you are not up to the task, you should consider hiring the services of an accountant to help you, particularly once your side gig starts to bring in larger amounts of money.

Let your boss know about your side gig. As long as you are not in direct competition with your employer's business, you should not hesitate to let them know about your side gig. Many employers actually welcome employees with a side gig, since this indicates that they have initiative. In addition, a side gig can teach an employee many valuable skills that they can bring to their jobs, which will improve their performance.

At the same time, however, you should make sure that you maintain a strict separation between your day job and your side gig. Never use office hours to work on your side business, and when you get home, leave your day job behind so you can focus on your side gig.

Find a support system. Since a side business will take up a lot of your time and energy, you should seek the help and support of friends and family. For example, you can ask them to watch the children while you're working on your side gig. You can assign your children some simple chores to free time that you can devote to your business.

In addition, you should also reach out to other entrepreneurs. They can provide you with valuable advice, as well as support, in your business. If possible, you should try looking for a mentor, someone who is already experienced in your field and who can provide you with guidance.

Make it professional. Treat your side gig as if it was a real business, otherwise you might not take it seriously enough and it will never grow into an actual business. One of the ways you can do this is by writing a business plan. A business plan is a blueprint of where you want your business to go in the future. In addition to your vision for your business, the plan should also talk about how you plan to market your business and how you are going to fund it, as well as measurable targets to meet over the next few months or years. For example, if you currently have one food cart, you can set a target of setting up a second one by the following year, and five by the end of your second year of operation.

In addition to helping you see your business in a more professional light, a business plan is also valuable once your enterprise starts to grow and you have to go to a bank or other lending agency to get a loan, or ask an investor to put money into your business. They will want to see your business plan so they'll know what your business is about and if they should help fund it.

Have fun. This is one of the most important tips in starting a side business. If you are not enjoying what you are doing, it will only be a drain on your energies. Your side business should be fun; otherwise what's the point?

What to Do Now

So, what's your passion?

Now it's your turn: choose one way to increase your income and make a concerted effort to make it happen. For instance, if you chose "take a college class," what will you do to make that a reality? Apply online? Register? How will

you pay for the class? Etc. Take the first step to increasing
your income by investing in yourself!

Chapter 9

Creating Passive Income

Creating passive income is truly a way out of financial bondage as the following benefits are to be enjoyed:

•   It is a recurring income. This means that once the investment is done, you can just wait monthly or yearly for your financial increase, without doing so much work or spending too much time on that investment. Technically, you can "retire" from your work (especially if the income is big) for it can be the source of your monthly expenditures.

•   Unlike in portfolio income, you have control over the investment in passive income. For example, you can decide whether you want to continue renting out the place or increase the rent or sell it.

•   Another great benefit is its tax rate. This has the most favorable tax treatment. Therefore, you can use the money that you saved from taxes for other investments.

•   The risks are often times low. Hence, it would also be safe to use borrowed money on this. There is no need to cash out a large amount of money. You can use the available money instead on other investments.

How to Make This Happen?

By now, you get the picture of why it is important to create passive income if you want to be financially free from today and even until you are gone (financial freedom for your family too). The main concern is how can you create a passive income? Here are 10 basic steps.

1.   Understand that financial success starts from within. You cannot be rich outwardly if you are not rich inside. How is this done? First, you need to renew your mind about money. Many of us have been taught or given the idea that becoming financially free is impossible. We grew up thinking that money is hard to get. Or worse, some of you might have been taught that money is the root of all evils, therefore one should not aspire to have them.

In order to be truly rich, we need to change our perception about money. We need to understand that money is neutral. It is neither good nor bad. The person who is handling the money is the one that gives personality to money. If the money is in the hands of a good person, then that will be used for good. That becomes good money then. Likewise, in the hands of a bad person, the money becomes bad because it will be used for bad things.

We also need to understand that acquiring money is not hard. It is easy. It can be done. It is time to remove the negative thoughts and confessions such as "It is so hard to become a millionaire" or "I don't always have enough money". Be positive. Think positive.

2.   Understand that everything is relative. What can make others happy will not automatically result to your happiness. This is very important to understand. So first, define what happiness is for you. Reflect on yourself. What is it that you really want or desire in life? Why is this important? Because your goals and plans should match. If your main desire is to become super rich, for example, the passive income that you need to create will be focused on that, on the creation of vast wealth. If your main goal is to be with your loved ones and just enjoy a simple life, then

your passive income will not be as aggressive but still profitable. The creation of the passive income will revolve around your plans and desires for life.

3.   Know yourself. This may sound silly but it is actually a very important step. There is no one-formula-that-works-for all out there. You have to find what fits you. The best thing to do before you create that passive income is to know what fits your personality, your future plans and your budget. For example, you enjoy blogging or doing a YouTube video. You can earn from them even after months or years that you have made them. The same thing is true when you author a book or compose a song. Stick to your passion and talents. After all, people are attracted to what is truly awesome or amazing. They would not support something that is mediocre or average.

Another example is if you like to bake and you have one special pastry that everybody loves. You can start with one shop. Hire people to bake for you and that's it. The shop can become famous without you baking the pastries yourself. That is how it was with KFC. And look where KFC is right now. So what it is that you truly enjoy doing? You can monetize that gift, without the need to leave your job.

You can imitate what a young man has done with his skill. He is gifted when it comes to investing in stocks. He started a website where people can subscribe to him (for a minimum charge per month) and he shares to them tips and guidelines in investing in stocks. It became popular because he has the talent to make the confusing world of investing easy to understand. He actually became a millionaire (not only from the stocks he invested) but from the subscription of millions of people because this is a "need" for many people. This brings us to the next step.

4.   Find a need. There would always be a need for many people. Be open for opportunities. Look around you. Oftentimes, these opportunities appear so simple that many people miss them. Look at yourself. What it is that you truly need? From there, you can design something that can create passive income for you. It does not have to be very important. It could be the little things.

Take the case of a young child who was frustrated with her gloves during wintertime. Why? She needed to remove the gloves to type in her cellphone, to button her clothes or play with her toys. Then she would wear them back because of the cold weather. She was irritated with the frequency and the need of removing and wearing the gloves over and over again. She solved the problem by cutting off the tips of the gloves, exposing the tips of her fingers. From then on, she was able to do other stuff even while wearing her gloves. Her mother thought it was a good idea and had it patented. She became a millionaire because of that.

There would always be a need. You just need to be alert to see these needs plus you have to be quick to answer them. As they say, need is the mother of invention.

5.   Create a plan. You can start by listing down your skills and talents. Then make a plan on how you can monetize your skill or gifting. Or if you are into investing, write down the amount that you need and where you will get that specific amount. Study about the different options that you have with investing and start investigating on the companies that you want to invest in.

Then, write down the plans. Why? Aside from the fact that various studies prove the effectiveness of writing the plans down, it is also a good way to create motivation for change. Have several copies of the written plan. Post or place them where you can see them always. The good places are:

a.   On the desk.

b.   In your wallet.

c.   Cellphone or laptop.

d.   Planner.

e.   On the wall of your bedroom

f.   On the mirror.

g.   On the door of your cabinet.

h.   On the door of the fridge.

This could be tiresome for some people but it is definitely a must. As they say, if you fail to plan, you plan to fail. So, do write down those plans right now and post them!

6.   Shop around. Investments have evolved. Formerly, you would simply have a health card or something so specific. Nowadays, these health cards come with investment opportunities on them. The same is true with life plans or insurances. Look at your options and compare the different companies. Check which investment and company suit you best. Interview different agents. Ask about their products. Check out the online forums too.

When you have finally chosen and bought the financially stable, there is something more that you could do. To help you save more, direct the income of these investments into buying more products or, to put it simply, re-invest the interest. This is known as the compounding interest which Albert Einstein himself consider as the eighth wonder of the world. This simply means that the money or interest that you earned goes back into investing. The more you do this, the higher your money gets.

7. Look around. What do you have? Do you have an extra space that you can use to earn? Maybe you can clean your garage and convert it into a room for one or two renters. Or, maybe you have a complete set of photography equipment that you do not want to give up. You can have your cake (meaning keep your precious photography equipment) and eat it too (earn from it by renting it out to others). Or, maybe there is an opening for a space that you can rent out to start your small business? Always be on the lookout on what could be profitable.

8. Be serious and yet treat passive income like a game. Creating passive income is a serious matter; however, this should be treated as a game. How? Let's take the computer game Mario for example. Mario has a princess to rescue as his final mission. What is your mission? If you know your mission, you will not be distracted with other things. You will be focused on achieving the mission.

Next, in order to earn coins (which Mario needs for his mission) he works and gets those coins. In the same manner, you need to have a job that will generate the income that you need for your everyday expenses, too. Some people commit the mistake of leaving their jobs when they have passive incomes already. You will get to that stage but not during the early years of having passive incomes.

Then, Mario goes to a different level once the goal has been reached. You also have to go to the next level of your investment. Do not be stuck on your level of investment. Move ahead. Move forward.

Along the way, there are many hindrances to Mario's target of rescuing the princess. The same things can happen to you as well. There would be hindrances to your journey to financial freedom. But you have to go on. You have to continue.

When the princess is rescued, the game ends. However, there is always another game available. The same holds true for you. Do not stop investing or creating passive incomes just because the mission has been accomplished already. Look for other investments to take.

9.   Remain positive. There will be hard times. There will be failures. These things are expected. They happen even to the best business people. So be ready for them. Failures are events in life. They do not define who you really are. The best thing that you can do is to keep that enthusiasm and positive attitude. Do not lose hope. Imagine yourself getting out of those difficult situations. Visualize yourself as successful.

10.   Passive income needs patience. Sometimes the return on income is low, just like in stocks. However, with time, this can grow into large amounts. Generating passive income does not take place overnight. It is like a seed. You need to watch over it and take good care of it. You need to be knowledgeable on how to care for it. You have to believe that someday it will cause you to reap multiple harvests. It would cause you to receive so much more from what you have invested.

Some points to remember

•   Passive income does not mean that there is no effort involved; rather that, if you've done your job properly, you have reduced the amount of effort needed to continue earning income regularly. Once you've set up your business and started earning passive income, however, you should not be complaisant but instead, constantly strive to improve your business. Keep in mind that business is very competitive and unless you are willing to constantly try to do better to serve your customers, you will lose your place and eventually your income will dry up.

• When your passive income is generating money for you, reinvest. Do not stop creating passive income. Some people tend to be lax when they have reached their goals. You can be content but not satisfied.

• Keep on developing yourself. Keep on learning. Keep your eyes open for new opportunities. Do not be narrow-minded. What has worked before may not be applicable for today. Innovate. Reinvent yourself. Learning is a lifetime process. There is always something to be learned. The moment you stop learning is the moment you stop growing and living.

• Do not be too dependent on that chicken that lays the golden egg. Remember that story? The farmer was at first happy with the golden egg that he gets every day from his chicken. But then, he gets impatient. He does not like to have one golden egg per day only. He wants many eggs and he wants them now. So, he starts to think that he can get all the eggs at once if he will kill the chicken that lays the eggs. He did and he opened her up. Alas! There were no golden eggs inside the chicken. And since the chicken is dead, the eggs stopped from coming. If only the farmer allowed more golden eggs to hatch and thus have more chickens laying golden eggs, that would have been a far better story.

As an investor, you should learn from this story. Of course, the first lesson is not to kill the chicken that is laying the golden egg. Instead, take good care of it. However, you can do more than that. Continue to look for other chickens that can lay golden eggs. How is this true in real life? For example, if one investment is doing well, do not put all your investment capital or money in that business. Diversify. If you are into stocks, divide your investments into several companies. If one investment fails, the success of the other investments can offset the loss.

• Another important thing to remember that our parents have not emphasized to us is the importance of giving back what has been given to us. We need to share our blessings to others, too. This falls under the category of passive income because you will reap a harvest long after you have planted your seed (finances) to others who have no ability to pay you back.

How is this possible? There is really no explanation. The universe was just designed this way. Take breathing for example. If you will just inhale oxygen and will not give off carbon dioxide, you will not survive. There is a time for giving and there is a time for receiving. It is not taking and taking from others only. You have to give and share, too. By doing so, you will find yourself getting richer and richer, not only in terms of finances, but even of friendships and relationships.

•   Lastly, passive income does not literally mean that you will be passive or inactive about your income. Yes, the idea is to have an income-generating activity or idea that does not require you to spend so much time and effort. However, the key word there is "so much". It simply means that time and effort would still be needed although not as much as you spend in a regular job.

In passive income, the effort is put in up-front, meaning that you work to set up the business so that, once it is up and running, you can basically just harvest the fruits of your labors. For example, when generating passive income from rental property, the effort is exerted in choosing the right property, applying for a loan to buy them, fixing up the property and screening tenants, so that once it is occupied, you can just collect the rent without doing too much work.

In addition, you are expected to be knowledgeable about your investments. You are expected to monitor and assess your investment regularly. You should be concerned with the investment. You should plan on how to improve it. Just like a plant, it will die if it is left on its own. It needs water, sunshine, fertilizer and other things as well. Your investment needs you to care for it too, however little that may be.

For example, once you have filled your investment portfolio with stocks, bonds or other types of investments, you cannot just leave it alone to accumulate value. You need to review the portfolio periodically to adjust your holdings. For example, you need to ask: Should I buy more stock? Should I sell shares of one stock and buy more shares of another? Should I reduce my holdings in stocks and increase my bond holdings? Should I invest in other investment types?

What To Do Now

You can create those passive incomes that would suit your personality and time. You have what it takes to be successful. You just need to be alert and ready for opportunities. Better yet, do not wait for those opportunities. Create these opportunities. As the successful people say, "Do not wait for things to happen. Instead, make things happen."

Creating passive income should be the goal of every one. It is a way to becoming financially stable. It is not an impossible endeavor. You can do it.

Conclusion

Our parents may have given us wrong ideas about money. It was not their fault. They have learned how to handle (or more appropriately, mishandle) money from their parents, too. If you grew up thinking these thoughts, "Money is hard to get" or "It is not safe to invest" then you will struggle with finances all your life. Renew your mind today. Believe that acquiring lots of money is not hard to accomplish. Believe that you have what it takes to be rich and successful in life.

Apply the principles taught here in your life. These are tested and proven to be effective. Although they may seem difficult at first, just keep on doing them. They have worked for thousands of people already. These people are now millionaires and some are billionaires. These lessons will work in your life, too.

To sum up, these are the 10 things you need to do and financial freedom is yours for the taking.

1.   Remember to pay yourself first with all your increase. Use this formula: Income minus payment to self equals expenses. Do not go back to the old formula of Income minus expenses equal savings. If you would stick to the old formula, there would never be a savings for you. There would always be something to spend your money with – that black dress, the newest gadget, a dream vacation, and others.

2.   Have an emergency fund equivalent to at least 3 months of your budget. The ideal is up to one year of your budget. This way, even when something untoward or unexpected happens, there is a safety net that will catch you.

3.   Save and spend wisely. You can always enjoy life without the need to spend so much. You just need to be creative on accomplishing this.

4.   Control your debt. Do all that you can to get out of debt. If you need to remove some luxuries in life, like watching movies weekly or having that expensive coffee daily, then do so. Sacrifice a little until all your debts are

fully paid. Then, refrain from getting into debt again. One secret shared by a millionaire is this: buy cash whenever possible. If you do not have the money to buy something you like, then wait till you have the money to do so. Do not use your credit card to finance your "wants" in life.

5.   Have a good credit history. Build your credit. This will help you in your future investments, especially if you need to borrow money from the banks. Control the way you use your credit card. If you think that you still need self-control, then refrain from using your credit card first. Do not bring it with you when you are shopping. Some credit card companies have an option of setting the exact amount you can spend only in a month. When you exceed the budget, the credit card will not allow you to spend more.

6.   Remember the "three buckets rule" when you invest your money. These are the security bucket, growth bucket and the dream bucket.

7.   Invest, invest, and invest. You cannot get rich by being an employee all your life. You need to invest.

8.   Increase your income. Learn the different types of incomes and the different ways to earn.

9.   Put up a business. Monetize your skill and gift.

10.　　Create passive income. Let money work for you and not the other way around. Earn even while you are sleeping.

Be free from the bondage of lack. You can be rich and successful in life. There is a way out of poverty. Obtain financial freedom today!

P.S. Can you please help me out!

If you enjoy this book and feel it has added value to your life in any way, please take the time to share your thoughts and post a review on Amazon. It'd be greatly appreciated!

A revolutionary productivity booster for your business

Would you like to speed up your work progress?

Hello,

Do you find yourself procrastinating and wasting precious time? Are you in need of help in managing your time so that you can make the best out of all your endeavors? Need assistance in taking control of your business, and moving towards your goals? Have you tried solving the above issues but to no avail?

Are you looking to strengthen a current business or set the proper foundation for one you are planning to start?

If you answer "YES" to any of these questions, we've got something amazing for you!

Whether you are a current business owner or someone planning to start a business soon, we can only help you if you are willing to take the steps needed to ensure your business is successful for many years to come. Running a business isn't about doing one thing right but being able to handle many things without dropping the ball.

A business is only as good as its everyday operation. Even if your sales are a steady stream of profit, a business lacking organization and an obvious handle on the day-to-day is unequipped to handle a steady stream. This is no different than asking someone to remind you of this date or that event when their system of operation is jotting notes on their skin: sure, they may remember to check the note but most likely it will get lost within the clutter and lack of system they rely on.

Now, I'm not saying that your business is unorganized to this point; I'm saying that any aspect where organization is an issue is a problem that could cause serious consequences in the near future. And this is why I am offering a simple video course for business owners to help you ensure that you have a handle in all aspects!

This video course will transform your business, guaranteed!

<u>CLICK HERE</u> to grab it today.

Don't forget to sign up for our **book club newsletter** where you can get your hands on some amazing books to skyrocket your business.

<u>CLICK HERE</u> to sign up!

Regards!

www.ingramcontent.com/pod-product-compliance
Lightning Source LLC
Chambersburg PA
CBHW060350190526
45169CB00002B/550